COUNTRIES

Popcorn

China

D0178189

Alice Harman

Explore the world with Popcorn - your complete first non-fiction library.

Look out for more titles in the Popcorn range. All books have the same format of simple text and striking images. Text is carefully matched to the pictures to help readers to identify and understand key vocabulary. www.waylandbooks.co.uk/popcorn

Published in paperback in 2013 by Wayland
Copyright © Wayland 2013

Wayland
Hachette Children's Books
338 Euston Road
London NW1 3BH

Wayland Australia
Level 17/207 Kent Street
Sydney NSW 2000

Produced for Wayland by
White-Thomson Publishing Ltd
www.wtpub.co.uk
+44 (0)843 208 7460

Editor: Alice Harman
Designer: Clare Nicholas
Picture researcher: Alice Harman
Series consultant: Kate Ruttle
Design concept: Paul Cherrill

British Library Cataloging in Publication Data
Harman, Alice
    China. -- (Countries)(Popcorn)
    1. China--Juvenile literature.
    I. Title II. Series
    915.1-dc23
ISBN: 978 0 7502 7920 8

10 9 8 7 6 5 4 3 2 1

Wayland is a division of Hachette Children's Books,
an Hachette UK company.
www.hachette.co.uk

Printed and bound in Malaysia

Picture and illustration credits: Peter Bull Art Studio: 23; Stefan Chabluk: 4; Shutterstock.com: Izmael 1, sunxuejun 5, cozyta 7, Fedor Selivanov 8, SEASUN 9, claudiozaccherini 10, beboy 2/11, huyangshu 12, Hung Chung Chih 13, 15, Bartlomiej Magierowski 14, Shcherbakov Ilya 16(t), bonchan 16(m), Brian Kim Photography 16(b), Monkey Business Images 17, smingcover/18, windmoon 19, szefei 20(t), GuoZhongHua 20(b), Cora Reed 21, Korionov 22; Wikimedia: Svy123/Kevin Mayea 6.

Every effort has been made to clear copyright. Should there be any inadvertent omission, please apply to the publisher for rectification.

 Contents

Where is China?

Here is a map of China. China is in East Asia. It is the fourth largest country in the world.

ASIA

Russia

Mongolia

Uzbekistan

Kyrgyzstan

G o b i
D e s e r t

North Korea

South Korea

Beijing

Yellow Sea

Kashgar

Tajikistan

Afghanistan

▲ K2

Pakistan

CHINA

Shanghai

East China Sea

River Yangtze

Nepal

Bhutan

India

Bangladesh

Guangzhou

Hong Kong

Pacific Ocean

Myanmar

Vietnam

Laos

South China Sea

Thailand

Beijing is the capital of China.
It is in the north of the country.
Beijing is one of the biggest cities
in the world.

Beijing has many new, tall buildings where people work in offices.

Around 20 million people live in Beijing.

Land and sea

The east of China is mostly quite low and flat, with hills and grasslands. Huge areas of desert spread across northern China. In the south-west, there are many high mountains.

K2, the second highest mountain in the world, is on China's border with Pakistan.

Eastern China has a very long coastline, with lots of small islands. The water can be very polluted, especially in areas near to cities such as Hong Kong.

Tourists take trips from Hong Kong in traditional Chinese boats called junks.

The weather

China is a huge country so it has very different weather in each area. In most parts of China, the weather is hot and rainy from May until October.

In summer, people from the cities head for China's sunny, sandy beaches.

Winter in China is between December and March. It is cold and dry in most of the country through the winter. In the north, the winter is much colder than in the south.

Roads to small villages are sometimes blocked by snow in winter.

Town and country

Cities in China are growing very quickly. People move from the countryside to find work in the cities.

The city of Shanghai is home to 17 million people.

People in the countryside often work on farms. They grow crops to feed the 1.4 billion people in China.

Rice is planted in flooded fields.

China grows more food than any other country in the world.

 Homes

China's city centres are often quite crowded. Many people choose to live further out of the centre, where houses are larger.

Lots of new houses are built every year to keep up with China's growing population.

Chinese houses in villages are traditionally made of wood. They have wide, pointed roofs and long, narrow balconies.

In villages high in the mountains, people build their houses into the steep slopes.

 Shopping

China has many large, new shopping centres in its towns and cities. They have stores from all over the world where people can buy things such as food, clothes and electronics.

Shangxiajiu is a famous shopping street in Guanzhou with more than 300 stores.

The two largest shopping centres in the world are in China.

China has many street markets that sell fresh food and cooked dishes. There are markets throughout the country, in big cities and small villages.

People sometimes carry home the food they have bought in large baskets on their back.

Food

Most areas of China have their own traditional style of cooking. Chinese food is normally eaten with chopsticks.

Chow mein is a dish of fried noodles cooked with any spices, vegetables, meat or seafood.

Fried rice with vegetables is a popular dish, served with a spoon but eaten with chopsticks.

Chinese cooking has opposite tastes in the same meal. Some dishes might be sweet and sour, others might have a spicy sauce but plain noodles.

A traditional Chinese meal includes many small dishes of different foods.

 # Sport

There are hundreds of different martial arts in China. Many of these are now popular around the world.

More than 200 million people in China do tai chi, an ancient martial art.

Lots of Chinese children learn martial arts at school or at summer camps.

Dragon boats have been made and raced in China for more than 2,000 years. Each long, wooden boat holds 22 people. One person hits a drum to help the team all row at the same time.

Teams racing in the Qu Yuan Cup decorate their boats with bright colours.

Holidays and festivals

The Moon Festival, also called the Mid-Autumn Festival, celebrates the harvest in September or October each year.

Mooncakes are special pastries with a sweet filling inside.

People watch street parades of huge paper lanterns in all shapes and colours.

Chinese New Year is the biggest festival in China. It lasts for 15 days in January and February. During this time, families and friends eat meals together and give gifts.

In Chinese New Year parades, the colour red means good luck.

Each Chinese year is linked with an animal such as the rabbit, the snake or the tiger.

Speak Mandarin!

There are many Chinese languages. Mandarin is spoken by the largest number of people, about 850 million. The sounds that make up some Mandarin words are written below.

Nee how	Hello
Tsy-jeean	Goodbye
Wo jee-ow …	My name is…
Tsun-mee yang?	How are you?
Chying	Please
Syeh-syeh	Thank you
Dway	Yes
Boo dway	No

The big golden star on China's flag stands for its government, and the four smaller stars are for its people.

Make a dragon puppet

You will need:
- Coloured paper or card • Scissors
- Glue • A length of ribbon
- Two lolly sticks
- A black pen

In China, dragons mean good luck and strength. At Chinese New Year, dancers hold up huge dragon puppets in parades.

1. Use the black pen to copy these shapes onto coloured paper or card. The dragon's head should be the biggest shape.

2. Stick the other shapes onto the head and tail. Draw eyes and nostrils on the dragon using the black pen.

3. Stick one end of the ribbon to the back of the dragon's head. Stick the other end to the back of its tail.

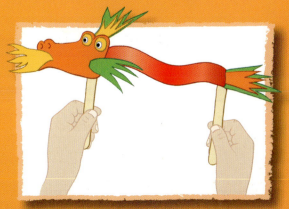

4. Stick one lolly stick onto the back of the dragon's head, and another onto the back of its tail. Now you can hold your puppet up and make it move!

Visit our website to download larger, printable templates for this project.
www.waylandbooks.co.uk/popcorn

23

Glossary

balcony an outdoor area on the side of a building, with a wall around it

border the line between two countries

capital the city where the government of the country meets

chopsticks thin sticks used for eating, especially in Asia

crops plants grown on a farm

electronics objects such as televisions and music players, which use electricity

flooded covered with water

harvest when a farmer's crops are fully grown, and are gathered to be eaten or sold

martial art an activity based on defending yourself when someone is trying to hurt you

office a room or building where people work

polluted containing waste, and therefore dirty and unhealthy

population the number of people living in a place, such as a country

Index